Cello Time Joggers

Piano accompaniment book

Kathy and David Blackwell

T0071030

Teacher's note
These piano parts are written to accompany the tunes in *Cello Time Joggers*. They are an alternative to the cello duet accompaniments or CD, and are not designed to be used with those items.

Kathy and David Blackwell

MUSIC DEPARTMENT

OXFORD
UNIVERSITY PRESS

Contents

2.	Under arrest!	1
4.	Down up	2
6.	Fast lane	3
7.	In flight	4
8.	Lift off!	5
9.	Katie's waltz	6
11.	Rhythm fever	7
12.	Here it comes!	8
13.	Tap dancer	9
14.	So there!	10
15.	Rowing boat	11
17.	C string boogie	12
18.	Travellin' slow	13
19.	Tiptoe, boo!	14
20.	Lazy cowboy	16
22.	City lights	17
23.	Clare's song	18
25.	Chinese garden	20
26.	Summer sun	21
27.	On the prowl	22
29.	Ready, steady, go now!	23
30.	Happy go lucky	24
32.	Listen to the rhythm	26
33.	Cattle ranch blues	27
34.	In the groove	28
35.	Stamping dance	29
36.	Walking bass	30
38.	Runaway train	31
39.	Distant bells	32
40.	Lazy scale	33
41.	The old castle	34
42.	Rocking horse	35
43.	Patrick's reel	36
44.	Calypso time	37
45.	Cello Time	38

Cello Time Joggers

piano accompaniment book

Kathy and David Blackwell

2. Under arrest!

KB & DB

The cello book contains several cello duets; these are unaccompanied and so not included here.

© Oxford University Press 2002 and 2014

Printed in Great Britain

OXFORD UNIVERSITY PRESS, MUSIC DEPARTMENT, GREAT CLARENDON STREET, OXFORD OX2 6DP

The Moral Rights of the Composers have been asserted. Photocopying this copyright material is ILLEGAL.

4. Down up

KB & DB

6. Fast lane

KB & DB

Possibly faster the second time through!

7. In flight

KB & DB

8. Lift off!

KB & DB

9. Katie's waltz

KB & DB

11. Rhythm fever

KB & DB

12. Here it comes!

KB & DB

13. Tap dancer

KB & DB

14. So there!

KB & DB

15. Rowing boat

KB & DB

17. C string boogie

KB & DB

18. Travellin' slow

KB & DB

19. Tiptoe, boo!

KB & DB

In the cello book this piece is notated without key signature.

13
p
sf
p
16
sf
p
sf
19
p
f
sub. p
f
23
sub. p
pp
sfz
Boo!
(shout)
8ve

20. Lazy cowboy

KB & DB

22. City lights

KB & DB

23. Clare's song

KB & DB

19
mp
mp
23
27
32
rit.
p
p

25. Chinese garden

KB & DB

26. Summer sun

KB & DB

27. On the prowl

KB & DB

29. Ready, steady, go now!

KB & DB

30. Happy go lucky (for Iain)

KB & DB

19
f
f
23
28
32
ff
ff

32. Listen to the rhythm

KB & DB

The repeat is written out in full in the cello part, which also includes alternative names for note-values.

33. Cattle ranch blues

KB & DB

34. In the groove

KB & DB

35. Stamping dance

Czech.

36. Walking bass

KB & DB

38. Runaway train

KB & DB

The music is written out in full in the cello part.

39. Distant bells

KB & DB

40. Lazy scale

KB & DB

41. The old castle

KB & DB

42. Rocking horse

KB & DB

43. Patrick's reel

KB & DB

44. Calypso time

KB & DB

45. Cello Time

KB & DB

17
1.
mp
19b
2.
pizz.
Fine
mp
23
cresc.
cresc.
26
mf
mf
rit.
D.𝄋 al Fine